D1293819

Let's Be Social

Meet Your Neighborhood

by L. L. Owens
illustrated by Chris Davidson

Content Consultant
M. A. Brennan
Assistant Professor, Community Development
Department of Family, Youth, and Community Sciences
University of Florida

SEAFORD PUBLIC LIBRARY
SEAFORD, NY 11783

magic
wagon

visit us at www.abdopublishing.com

Published by Magic Wagon, a division of the ABDO Group, 8000 West 78th Street, Edina, Minnesota 55439. Copyright © 2011 by Abdo Consulting Group, Inc. International copyrights reserved in all countries. All rights reserved. No part of this book may be reproduced in any form without written permission from the publisher.

Looking Glass Library™ is a trademark and logo of Magic Wagon.

Printed in the United States of America, North Mankato, Minnesota.
012010
092010

 THIS BOOK CONTAINS AT LEAST 10% RECYCLED MATERIALS.

Text by L. L. Owens
Illustrations by Chris Davidson
Edited by Mari Kesselring
Interior layout and design by Becky Daum
Cover design by Becky Daum

Library of Congress Cataloging-in-Publication Data
Owens, L. L.
  Meet your neighborhood / by L.L. Owens ; illustrated by Chris Davidson ; content consultant M. A. Brennan.
     p. cm. — (Let's be social)
  Includes index.
  ISBN 978-1-60270-803-7
  1. Neighborhoods—Juvenile literature. I. Davidson, Chris, 1974-
II. Title.
  HM761.O94 2011
  307.3'362—dc22
                                    2009048354

Table of Contents

What Is a Neighborhood?

Every city is made up of neighborhoods. In a big city, thousands of families live in one neighborhood. A neighborhood in a small town has just a few homes. In very small towns there is only one neighborhood.

A neighborhood has homes, buildings, streets, and people. All of these are parts of a neighborhood.

A neighborhood might have:
a grocery store, a gas station,
a swimming pool, a courthouse,
a fire station, a bank, a movie
theater, places of worship, or
a dentist office.

A neighborhood has many kinds of homes. A house is meant for one family. A duplex is a house split into two homes. One family lives in each home. Town houses are a row of houses connected to each other.

Some neighborhoods have apartment buildings. Many families live in a building. Each apartment is a home.

Neighborhoods have businesses. They help the people living there.

A neighborhood often has a library and a post office. People use the library to get books. People can send and receive mail at the post office.

A hospital is an important part of a neighborhood. In 1751, the first U.S. hospital was founded in the Olde City neighborhood of Philadelphia, Pennsylvania.

The people in a neighborhood are called neighbors. They make the neighborhood special.

Nathan lives in a small neighborhood. He knows all his neighbors. If Nathan lived in a big neighborhood, he would not know everyone.

Types of Neighborhoods

Neighborhoods come in all shapes and sizes. Dylan and his mother live in a neighborhood that fits the needs of their lifestyle. Neighborhoods change to fit people's needs. Dylan welcomes the good changes.

A neighborhood of young families is different from one where many older people live. These two groups have different needs. Their neighborhoods meet those needs.

Mariah and her family live in a neighborhood that is family-centered. It has houses with yards, quiet streets, and a playground. Many of Mariah's neighbors are kids, too!

No two neighborhoods are exactly the same. Neighborhoods are always changing.

18

Theo and his family live in the city. The houses are close to the street. Bus stops line the street. Theo's neighborhood has a museum and coffee shops.

Some neighborhoods have names. A name helps identify an area. It usually relates to a location, local business, event, landmark, or person.

The Garcia family's neighborhood is called Johnson Beach. It might be named after an early settler. And it is near the ocean.

A few U.S. neighborhoods:
- Lincoln Park in Chicago, Illinois
- Pioneer Square in Seattle, Washington
- Chinatown in San Francisco, California

Neighborhood Happenings

Many people live in Jason's neighborhood. His family has lived there for a long time. It's where his grandparents grew up!

People spend a lot of time in their neighborhoods. They play. They eat. They make friends. They do just about everything!

Megan's neighborhood is a big part of her life. She notices when it changes.

Megan and her mother like to greet new neighbors. Keeping their neighborhood safe and clean matters to them. So does being friendly to their neighbors.

FRAGILE

FOR SALE
SOLD
NEW
NEIGHBOR

Luke helps make his neighborhood a great place. He gets to know his neighbors. Together, they make a small community.

Luke and his neighbors work together as a community. Good neighbors look out for each other.

Neighborhood events bring people together. Luke's neighborhood has a fun bike race every summer.

Strong neighborhoods are good for the people in them. People who are happy about where they live are likely to stay. Life is more enjoyable.

Good neighbors take care of their neighborhoods. They make the world a better place!

29

COMMUNITY

Neighborhood Project

You can make your neighborhood a better place by keeping it clean! Ask an adult to help you. Get a group of neighborhood friends together to pick up litter around the neighborhood. Try to include many of your neighbors.

You will need:

- gloves

- trash bags

- a dumpster

- rakes

- food and water for the volunteers

Fun Facts

- You can do an Internet search for famous birthplaces in your area. Maybe a U.S. president was born in your neighborhood!

- The Back Bay neighborhood in Boston, Massachusetts, is home to America's oldest public library.

Glossary

identify—to recognize and name.

landmark—a structure or a geographic feature that identifies a location.

lifestyle—way of life.

relate—to have a connection with something.

settler—a person who comes to live in a new place.

On the Web

To learn more about neighborhoods, visit ABDO Group online at **www.abdopublishing.com**. Web sites about neighborhoods are featured on our Book Links page. These links are routinely monitored and updated to provide the most current information available.

Index